Reflections of Love

33 Poems & Images Inspired by the Heart

Ron Vesci

PASSION STATEMENT

Getting "In Tune" with the Present Moment is a practice that cannot be overlooked, and unfortunately is, by the vast majority of people living today. Broken down to Its Primal Core, Presence is Vital to Happiness, True Happiness. Otherwise, we are consistently in a past or future reference point, which constricts our Being, and clogs the Universal Creative Flow that we ALL ARE. So my Intention is to help others on their Life Journey, by sharing my therapeutic process of Spontaneous Creative Connection. These poems Manifested through Breath and a Thoughtless Channel, and emerged within a 5-20 min time frame. The corresponding photos were also taken by me to help merge the Power of Nature into every equation, for WE ARE Nature. I've found through many years of Practice, my creativity has set me Free from the constraints of time, and has helped me live a predominantly Happy life. If I could just help one person ease their suffering through their own Creative Treasure Chest, and increase their Happiness, my Mission IS Accomplished.

Just Remember... YOU ARE the Master of Love...

The Conductor of Peace...

The Brilliant Magician...

So Manifest your Magic...

And So It IS...

Love is the cure, for your pain will keep giving birth to more pain until your eyes constantly exhale love as effortlessly as your body yields its scent.

~ RUMI

DEDICATED TO THE HIGHEST LOVE, THAT RESTS IN THE ALTARS OF EACH AND EVERY SOUL.

THE TEMPLE OF TRUTH THAT GUIDES OUR SPIRIT AND FEEDS OUR CREATIVITY...

EVERY MOMENT...

I GIVE THANKS...

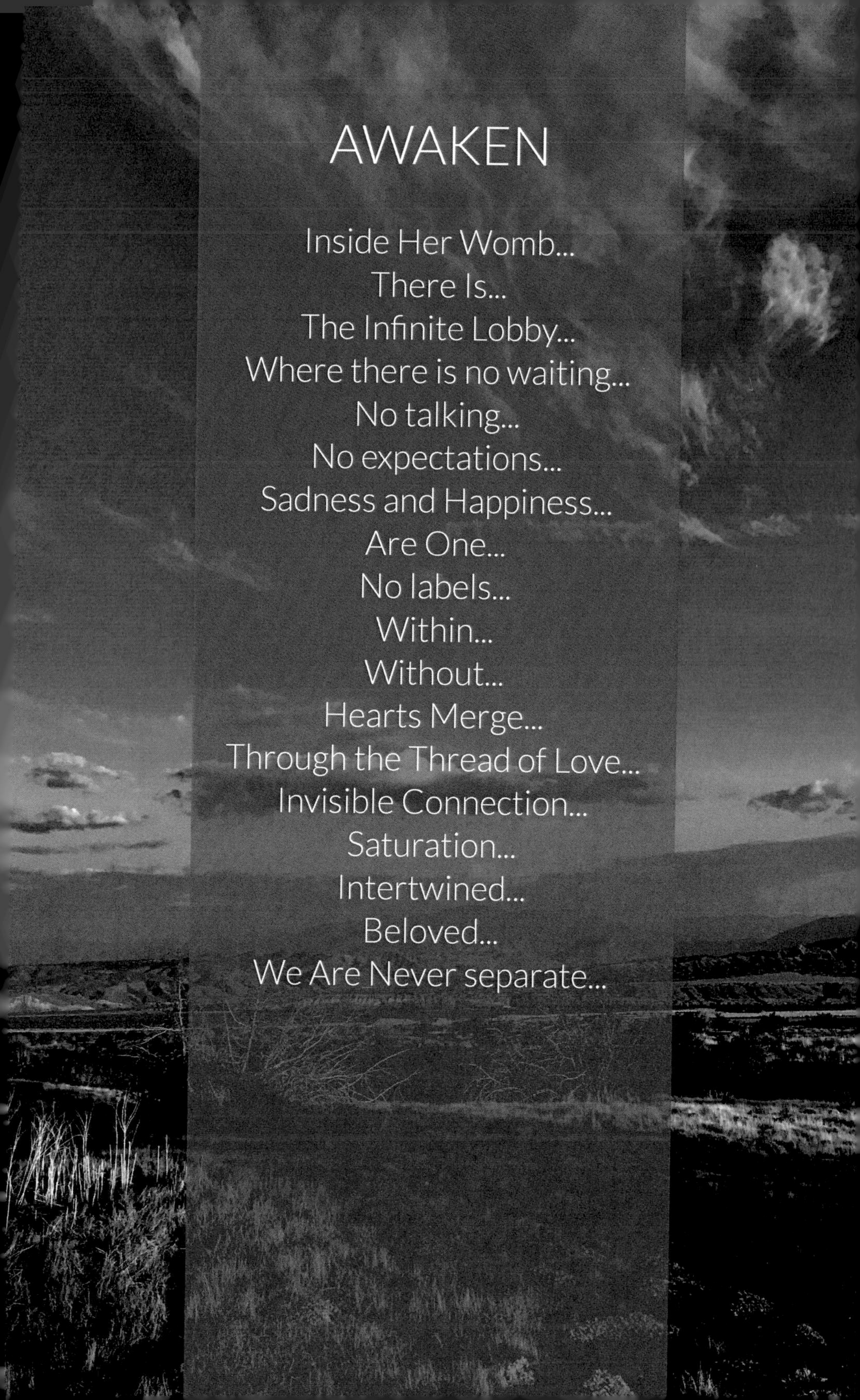
AWAKEN
Inside Her Womb...
There Is...
The Infinite Lobby...
Where there is no waiting...
No talking...
No expectations...
Sadness and Happiness...
Are One...
No labels...
Within...
Without...
Hearts Merge...
Through the Thread of Love...
Invisible Connection...
Saturation...
Intertwined...
Beloved...
We Are Never separate...

DO NOT PASS

BELIEF IS LIMITLESS

Inside the Breath...
Is Infinite Power...
Beyond Point of View...
Recognition...
Visibility...
The Omnipotent Seat...
That has NO destination...
No expectations...
Only Abundance...
Self-Realized Belief...
The Realization...
That we are the only ones...
Who can block our Dreams...
Once we Believe...
That IS what Will occur...
So Believe Big...
Believe Dynamically...
Believe Infinitely...
Because Belief...
Is Limitless...
Make It Magical...
Make It Heart Expanding...
You ARE the Magician...

BELOVED LIGHT

The clouds of time...
Drift by...
Opening the Mystery...
Unraveled...
Into the Omni...
Freedom...
Releases the grip...
Connecting...
Intuitively...
Inherent Beauty...
Flows...
With each Breath...
Merging...
Soaring...
In Love's Infinite Breeze...
The Gentle Whisper...
Of Now...
For You ARE...
The Beloved Light...

BRIGHT STAR

Visions of Your Face...
Open my Heart...
Like a Flower...
On a Brilliant Sunny Day...
Contemplation...
Of Our Infinite Love...
Is my Mainstay...
You ARE the Rock...
The Magical Healer...
That Knows no bounds...
You ARE the Music...
In my Soul...
The Magic...
In my Creations...
The Butterfly...
In my Nectar...
The Blue...
In my Sky...
No Beginning...
No Ending...
Just Love...
The Rainbow Hue...
That Heals All...
You ARE...
The Reflective Bright Star...

CLOUDS OF TRUTH

Inside the Master...
The Universe Patiently Waits...
Virtuously Embracing...
Every stumble...
Bad choice...
Road block...
Reassuring...
That every dark cloud...
Has a Purpose...
Professing...
Your Mastery...
Brilliance...
Perseverance...
Vision...
Find your Passion...
Live your Passion...
And All obstacles...
Will Be...
Clouds of Truth...

DIVINE PROPORTION

The Universe Calls...
Inside the Machine...
The Cosmic Mandala...
Of Life...
Draws me In...
To Her Heart...
Through the Layers of Love...
The stars seem separate...
But Reality proves Otherwise...
Interconnection...
High Speed Energy...
The Creative Master...
Hologram Essence...
Starlight Express...
Into Love's Black Hole...

EGOLESS BEAUTY
Standing Tall...
Flowing with Grace...
Her Essence...
Is Known to ALL...
Who See Her...
Not a word is spoken...
No thought perceived...
Only Her Being...
Magnificence...
Extraordinary Brilliance...
Grounded in Truth...
Proof...
Of Solitary Action...
Oneness...
That Connects...
Inside Love's Garden...
Egoless Beauty is Found...

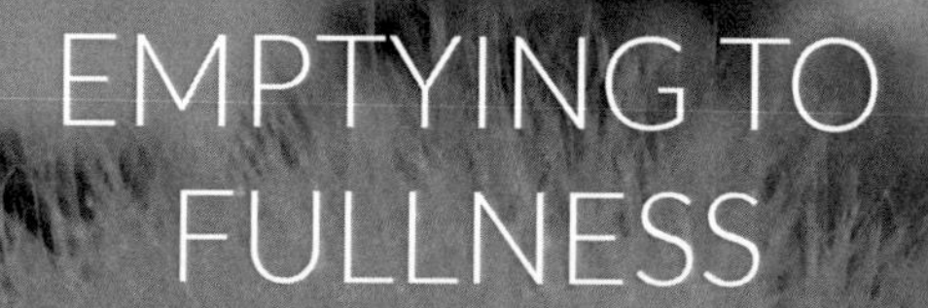

EMPTYING TO FULLNESS

Breathing In...
The Essence...
Releasing...
To the Magic of Peace...
Now...
Is the Medicine...
Love...
Is the Doctor...
You...
Are the Alchemist...
The Holy Trinity...
The Magician...
The Infinite Light...
That only dims...
When not Connected...
To Love...
Open...
The Window of your Heart...
And Fly Away...
Soar...
With Your Highest Self...
From the Seat...
Of Your Soul...

ENGINEER OF LOVE

In the Beginning...
Is the Heart...
The Magical Conductor...
Of Every Breath...
The Engineer...
Of Love...
Driving the machine...
Into each Intention...
Moment to Moment...
We Set our Sails...
Dance...
With a New Beginning...
A Present Outcome...
Cut the cords that constrict...
Meditate the chaos...
Disintegrate separation...
Climb In...
To the Universal Soul...
And Begin Again...

I look at your Face...
And See My Reflection...
Love...
Is In the Mirror...
Visions of time...
Only prolongs Truth...
We ARE ONE...
Stalks of fiber...
Obstruct the Pathway...
So it seems...
Merge...
Dance...
For time is our Friend...
If it doesn't define us...
Every Second...
IS Love...
If we Choose IT to BE...

FULL SPECTRUM RADIATION

Arms Wide Open...
The Sun...
Calls to my Heart...
I AM...
Not separate...
In my Infinite Cavern...
Grounded...
In Truth...
Pulsing...
In the shallow depths...
Of time...
Converging...
With Her Flowering Majesty...
Full Spectrum Radiation...
Ultimate Connection...
Linked Chain...
Love Train...
Rain...
On the Universal Terrain...
Your Soul Flower...
Is Released...

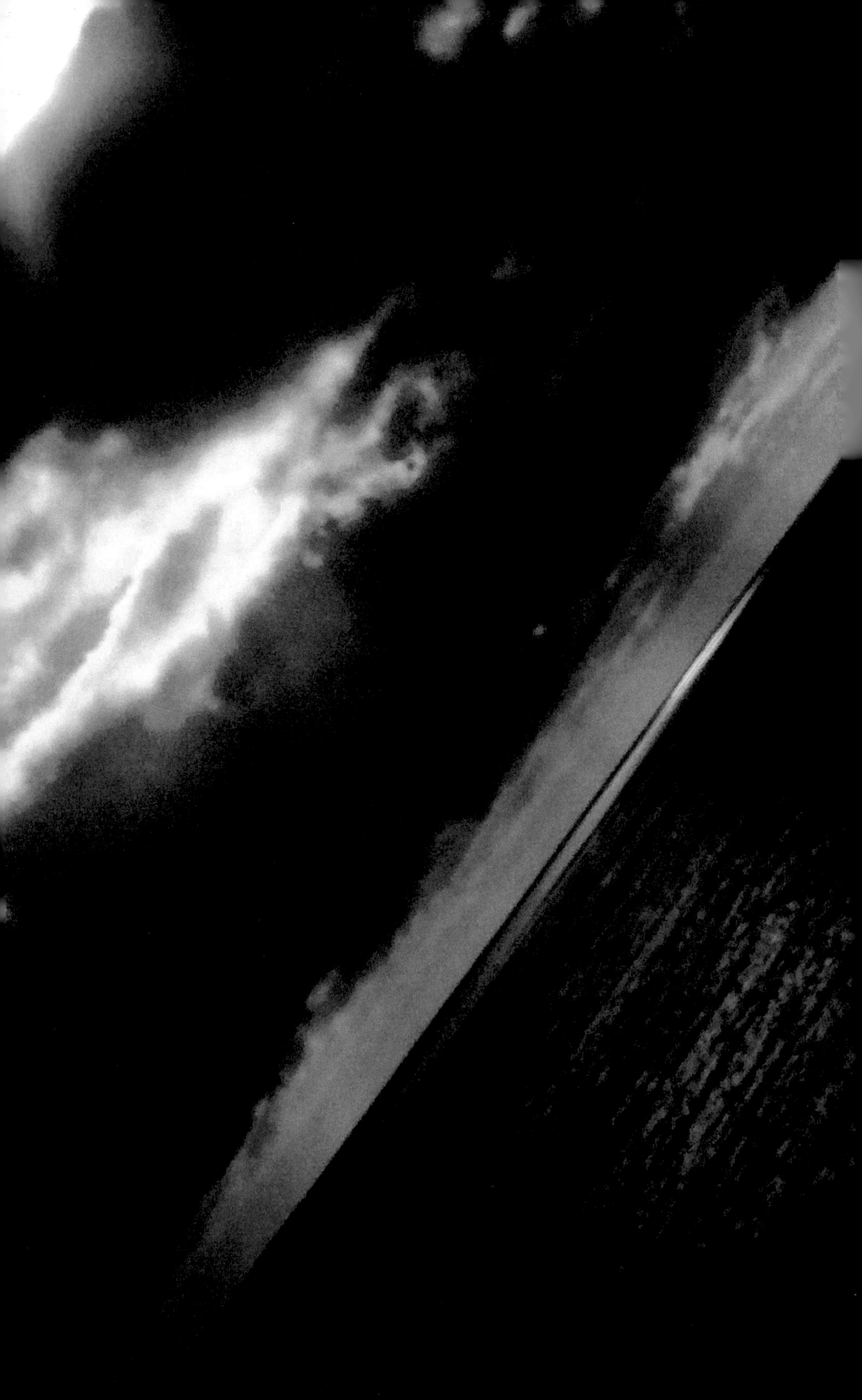

INVERSION

Balance...
The Light...
Creeps In...
From topside left...
Illuminate...
De-segregate...
Activate...
The Whole...
Ebbs and Flows...
In Divine Timing...
The Blank Canvas...
On the Great Creator's Wall...
Shimmers...
Beckons...
Reaches...
The Heights...
Of Your Love...
Co-Create...
Stimulate...
Disintegrate...
Into One Love...

JHANA
(Teaching)

The Drumming of time...
Flows...
Tapping the Vine...
Authenticity...
Drips of Love...
Feed the Master...
Heart Beats...
Rhythmic Breath...
Dance...
With the Present...
Merge...
Into the Now...
Release...

LAST IN LINE

Brilliance...
Is In each and every Breath...
How do you Dance?...
With Love?...
Humility? ...
Vulnerability?...
Compassion? ...
Gratitude? ...
Overcome division...
Oneness Overflow...
Unites...
The Infinite CO-OP...
Love's Corporation...
No difference...
Between a Beggar and a CEO...
We ALL Glow...
In the same Flow...
Wherever you ARE...
BLOOM!!...
Share your Omnipotent Fragrance...
Even if it appears...
You're Last in Line...
SHINE!!...
For there is NO order in Love...

The Greens and Blues of Now...
Hypnotize...
Fears...
Paralyze...
Institutionalize...
Love...
It's not below...
Or above...
It's In...
Your Reflection...
Heart Connection...
With Abundance...
Cut the cords...
That inhibit...
Dance with your Truth...
Flow...
Inside Love's Mothership...
The countdown...
To Now...
Three...
Two...
ONE...
Love...

MAGIC IN THE DISTANCE

The Mountain...
Calls to Me...
Shedding Its Beauty...
Into My Soul...
Sprinkling Its Wisdom...
Into the Universal Flow...
Coalescing...
To the Infinite Now...
The Oneness...
That Spans the Cosmos...
Yet...
Fuels Every Cell...
Every Breath...
Every Moment...
There is no separation...
Between the Mountain...
And Me...
Freedom...
Instantaneous Reflection...
Connection...
To the Infinite Now
Sparkling Presence...
Unified Essence...

MAGNIFIED MIST

Timeless...
Contemplation...
Connection...
Expansion...
From a Droplet...
To the Sea...
Ebbs and Flows...
Breathe In Peace...
Release...
The fear...
Leashed to Love...
The Essence...
We Are Made Of...
Smiling...
Mother's Tears of Joy...
Raining Down...
The Oneness...
That Washes Us Clean...
The Magnified Mist...
Showcasing Our Unity...
Through...
The Universal Veins of Love...
The Common Thread...
Consistently Weaving...
TRUTH...

MASTER'S REFLECTION

The hues...
Of life...
Infuse...
Confuse...
Mystify the mind...
But Only when separate...
The Veins of Love...
Connect...
Pulsing the Juice...
Of Now...
From shadows...
To Brightness...
Solitary Bliss...
Engulfing Infinity...
Tracks of Light...
Guide the Way...
To The Master's Reflection...
You...
Me...
US...

NEW BEGINNING

I Close my Eyes...
And Merge...
With All Directions...
Reflecting...
The Inner Essence...
Into Every Action...
Every Touch...
Fragrance...
Visionary Love...
Immersing Your Presence...
Reeling In...
From the Omnipotent Well...
Drink...
Bathe...
Laugh...
In the Ever Present...
New Beginning...

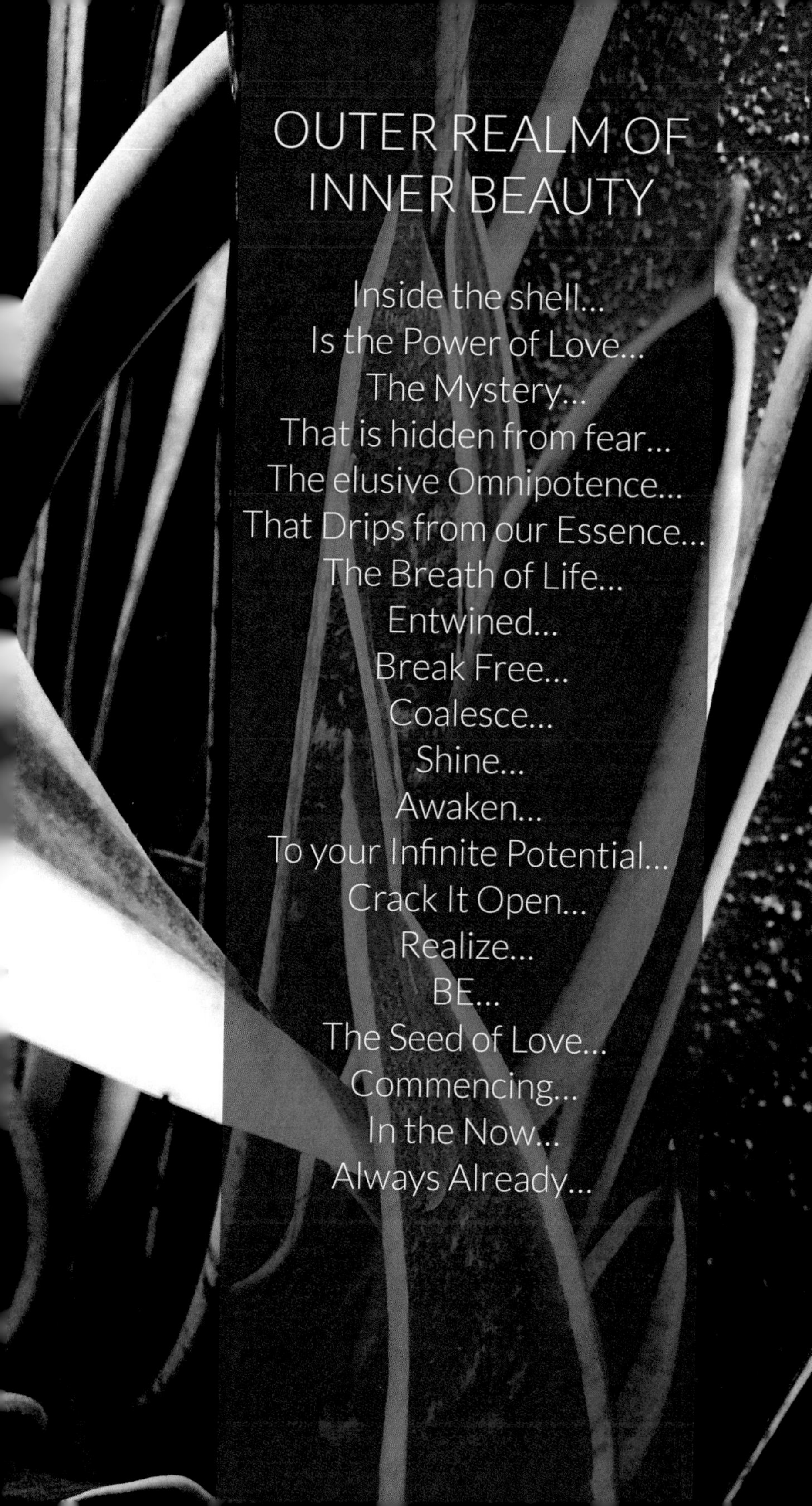

OUTER REALM OF INNER BEAUTY

Inside the shell...
Is the Power of Love...
The Mystery...
That is hidden from fear...
The elusive Omnipotence...
That Drips from our Essence...
The Breath of Life...
Entwined...
Break Free...
Coalesce...
Shine...
Awaken...
To your Infinite Potential...
Crack It Open...
Realize...
BE...
The Seed of Love...
Commencing...
In the Now...
Always Already...

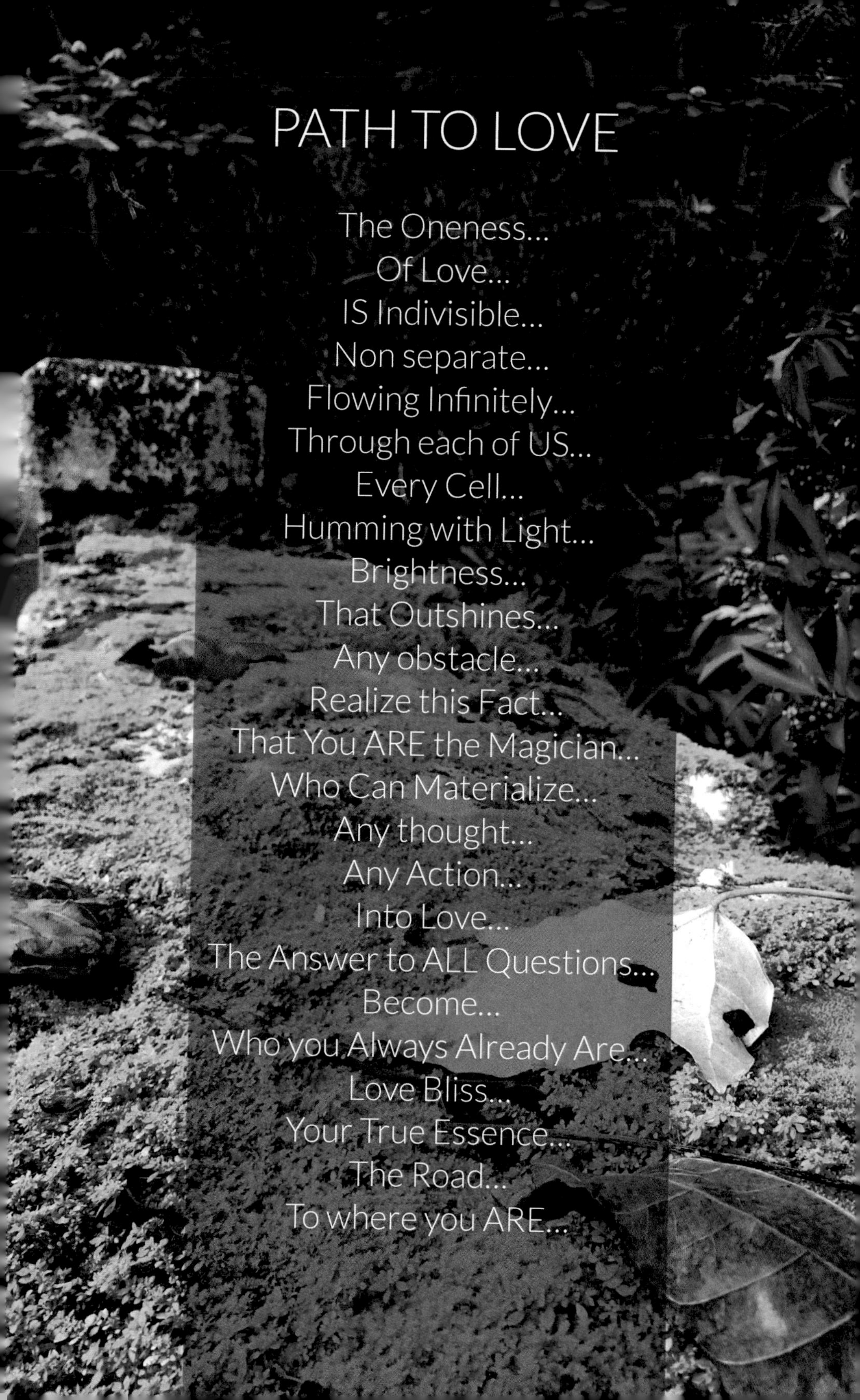
PATH TO LOVE
The Oneness...
Of Love...
IS Indivisible...
Non separate...
Flowing Infinitely...
Through each of US...
Every Cell...
Humming with Light...
Brightness...
That Outshines...
Any obstacle...
Realize this Fact...
That You ARE the Magician...
Who Can Materialize...
Any thought...
Any Action...
Into Love...
The Answer to ALL Questions...
Become...
Who you Always Already Are...
Love Bliss...
Your True Essence...
The Road...
To where you ARE...

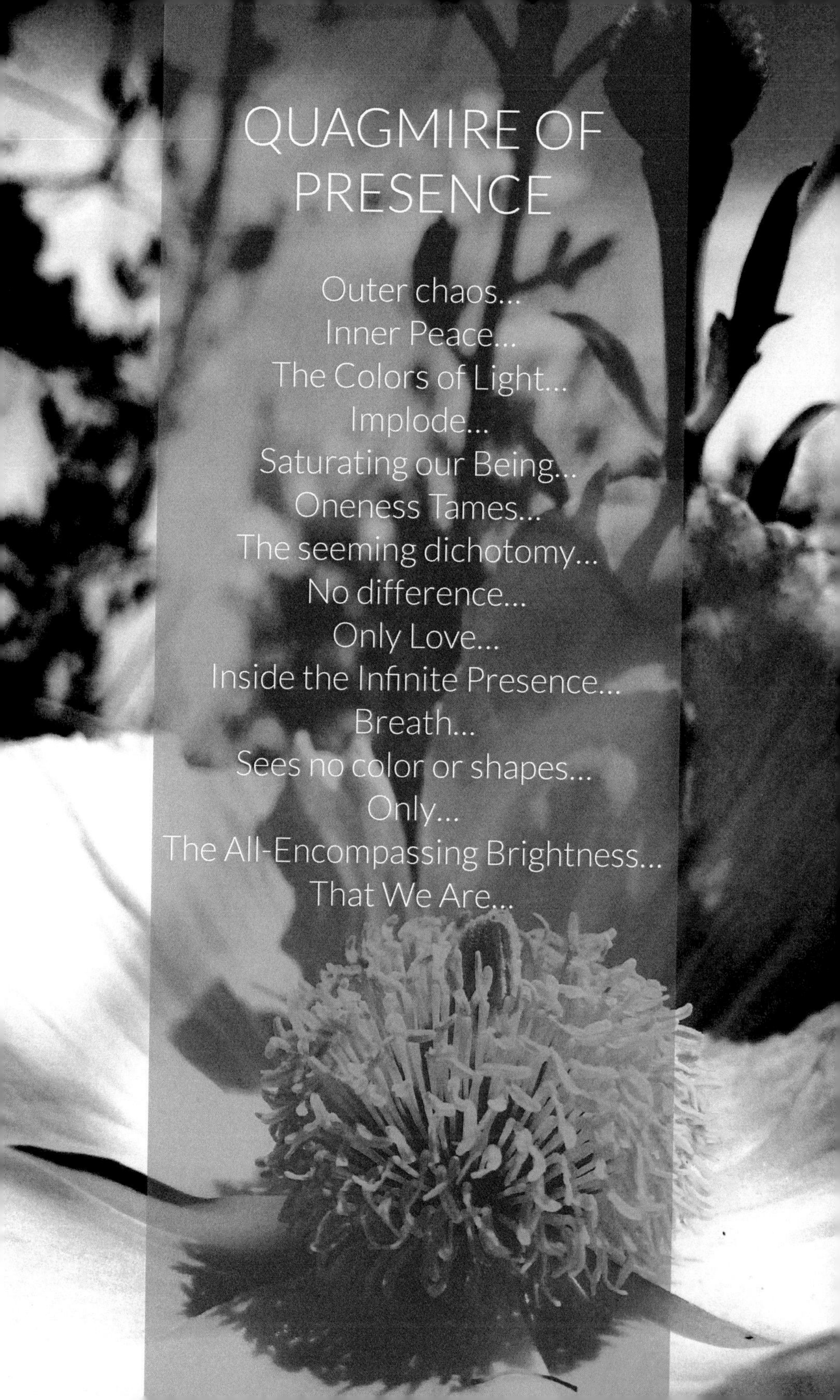

QUAGMIRE OF PRESENCE

Outer chaos...
Inner Peace...
The Colors of Light...
Implode...
Saturating our Being...
Oneness Tames...
The seeming dichotomy...
No difference...
Only Love...
Inside the Infinite Presence...
Breath...
Sees no color or shapes...
Only...
The All-Encompassing Brightness...
That We Are...

RADICAL RESONANCE

Release the Search...
Let it go...
Return...
To that Formless Place...
The Heart Space...
Where expectations vanish...
And Breath IS the Principal...
Things...
Indivisible...
Love...
Integral...
The Infinite Circle...
That leads to Now...
The Only Important place to Be...
Free...
From the search...
Resting...
In the Arms...
Of Love...

SACRED MIRROR

The Mystery of Life...
Is Reflected...
Through the Lens of Love...
The Infinite Eye...
The warrior's Heartbeat...
Intuitive Response...
Oneness...
With What Is...
The Breath...
The Unseen Beauty...
Perpetual Resonance...
That Knows Only Love...
Coalesce...
Into the sacred Mirror...

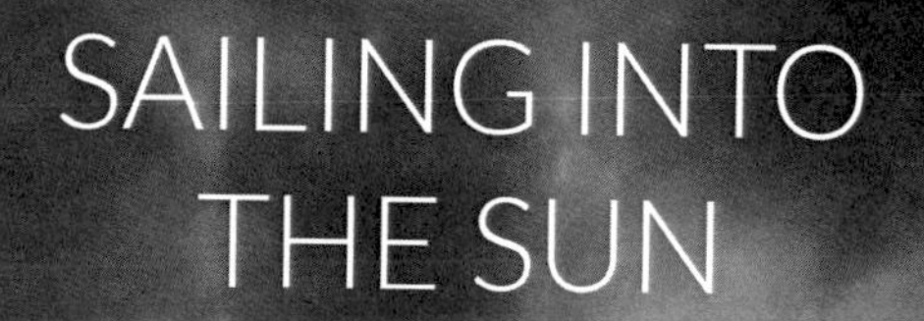

SAILING INTO THE SUN

Navigation...
From the Heart...
Reveals...
The Esoteric Magic...
Intimate Connection...
Waves of Truth...
Freedom Sessions...
Reflecting...
Infinite Delight...
Clouds of delusion...
Disintegrate...
Outshining...
Sailing...
Into the Sun...
Shine On Lovers...

SEAT OF LOVE

Inside the machine...
Is a Nothingness...
That Magnifies Truth...
By Releasing fear...
And Opening...
The Window of your Heart...
Melting...
Like snow...
On a warm winter day...
Interconnecting...
Basking...
Hand in Hand...
Kissing the Magic...
On the Universal Seat of Love...

SHIMMERING

In front of me...
The Blank Canvas...
Is Bright and Shimmering...
Looking into my Heart's Eye...
Gazing at my Intuition...
Merging with my Consciousness...
Vibrational Being...
Releases the grip...
Dissolving...
Into Creative Spontaneity...
Fly Away...
Like a Feather...
Dancing in the Sky...
Gently Arriving...
At each Moment...
ALL ABOARD!!...

THE BRIDGE ACROSS NOW

Inside the Mystic...
Is a Presence...
That Knows Only Love...
Flowing...
In the River of Truth...
Through Every Breath...
Every Heartbeat...
Every Living Being...
Nothing separates this Fact...
Except fear...
FEAR NOT!!...
For You Are the Mystic...
The Magic...
The Infinite River...
That IS...
The Sea of Love...

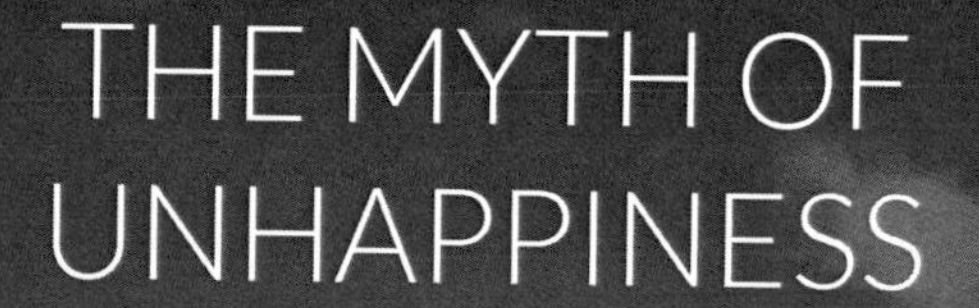

THE MYTH OF UNHAPPINESS

The Core of All...
Is Love...
Inside...
The mind-made shell...
Is Infinite Freedom...
Always Already Present...
Patiently Waiting...
For that Re-Connection...
The dark clouds and heavy rains...
Always Return to Blue Skies and Sun...
The Everpresent Clarity...
Only temporarily covered...
By earthly dramas...
Crack that shell...
Release...
Your Inner Light...
Love's Beacon...
Omnipotent Bliss...
Trumps...
The myth of unhappiness...

TIME

Separation...
Creates the barb in the wire...
The bigotry in the Love...
Chaos in the Peace...
How are you going to spend your time?...
The Masters say...
Merge with your Breath...
Become One with Your Truth...
Believe...
That You ARE...
Your Essence can Grow...
In ANY environment...
Be the Example...
Be Your Truth...
Nothing will Stop You...

WABI SABI

Self doubt...
Eases in...
Only to confuse...
Dead skin...
Reemerges...
With the Ether...
Begin Again...
Love's Cliché...
The Infinite Engine...
That Redefines...
Each Breath...
The Ebb and Flow...
Of Life...
Commences...
Your Truth...
The Soul's Fragrance...
Is Absolute...
And Has the Answers...
To All of Life's obstacles...
Release Contractions...
Breathe In...
And Begin Again...

WISPY ON THE ROCKS

Floating...
Weightlessly...
Prior To thought...
Enveloped in Breath...
Drunk on Love...
Blissful Intoxicant...
Releases our grip...
Dancing in Passion...
No limits...
No separation...
Only Abundance...
Outshining...
The precipice of time...
Enjoying...
Indulging...
In Another...
Wispy On the Rocks...

WITHIN-WITHOUT

The Seed of Life...
Beginning from Nothingness...
Open Petal...
Pedaling into Now...
The seeming upward spiral...
Piercing the Heavens...
The Clouds...
Are the beautiful illusion...
Transcending Truth...
The Flight Within...
Is the Beginning...
No thing...
Will bring...
Happiness...
Only Breath...

ACKNOWLEDGMENTS

My Heartfelt Gratitude goes out to my Mom and Herb, for Selflessly and Unconditionally shelling out their Love Consistently, I Love You with All of my Essence.

I also give thanks to Marci Rosen for her tireless creativity on designing this book... your unique Creative Depth brought a Higher Dimension to the layout of this book. Thank You my Love, You Are a Dear Friend and Mentor.

To ALL of my Unique and Wonderful friends and family (too many to name on this shallow page). You have a Deep Etching in my Heart and have shaped me into who I AM. I Give Ultimate Thanks!

Walk Into Now, with Gratitude, Compassion and Reflections of Love...

Moment to Moment...

And So It Is...

Kolya~

To my Best and most Consistent friend on earth during this lifetime, and possibly many others---

I love You Brother---

To many More to Come...

You are a True Gem my Brother....

Peace | Light | Love

[signature]

56111173R00042

Made in the USA
San Bernardino, CA
08 November 2017